Original title:

Petals in My Pocket

Copyright © 2025 Creative Arts Management OÜ
All rights reserved.

Author: Cassandra Whitaker
ISBN HARDBACK: 978-1-80581-933-2
ISBN PAPERBACK: 978-1-80581-460-3
ISBN EBOOK: 978-1-80581-933-2

Fragments of Flora

Tiny blooms fill my coat,
A surprise for every note.
In a pocket, a garden grows,
With whispers of laughter, it shows.

Petals tumble, a colorful mess,
When I walk, they dance and dress.
Like confetti from my whimsical dress,
Each step a floral happiness.

Tucked Away Blossoms

In my bag, a secret stash,
Little flowers, a wild clash.
Reaching for gum, I find a sprout,
Who knew joy could come about?

A sunflower peeks from my shoe,
Daisy chains making me blue.
With every rustle, a giggle slips,
Nature's laughter in my grips.

The Weight of Lavender Dreams

Lavender sprigs in my pockets cling,
They smell like summer, oh, what a swing!
Though I trip on their fragrance bold,
Each stumble tells tales yet untold.

A waltz of scents fills the air,
My friends wonder if I care.
But blooms have a way of brightening the load,
Even if it's wild, this flowery road.

Hidden Gardens of the Soul

In my heart, flowers bloom anew,
Surprises hiding, just like the dew.
While I ponder where they came from,
A chuckle escapes, like a drum.

With every mishap, petals fly,
"Where'd that rose go?" I wonder why.
In my soul's pockets, laughter sprouts,
Hidden gardens, no doubt, no doubts!

Petal Trails of Forgotten Youth

In shadows of laughter, we ran so free,
With pockets of blooms and a hint of glee.
Chasing the sun, we twirled in delight,
Now I find remnants tucked in at night.

Jokes were like blossoms that danced in the air,
Sticky and sweet, without a care.
Pockets bulging with nature's surprise,
Who knew that a flower could cause such a rise?

The Dance of Colors Within

Waltzing with hues in a midsummer breeze,
Colors erupting like playful bees.
A swirl of red, yellow, and blue,
Each petal's a giggle; my heart's in a stew.

I tripped on a violet, landed with flair,
Rolling in daisies, without a care.
Nature's confetti wrapped round my feet,
Causing a mess that feels oh-so sweet.

Nature's Keepsake of Softness

Fuzzy and bright, I collide with a bloom,
Softness in pockets, don't need any room.
A giggle escapes as I prance through fields,
Nature's own secrets, my heart always yields.

Laughter and petals, a curious blend,
Whenever I trip, those petals descend.
Jokes on my clothes, a floral disguise,
With every tumble, more nature complies.

Enchanted Fragments of Nature

Tiny confetti from the trees above,
Sprinkles of wonder, like whispers of love.
I gather them up, these bright little flakes,
Who knew nature smiles when it rains and shakes?

A bouquet of mischief in pockets I stash,
Each bloom a tickle, a gentle little splash.
Magic awaits in each quirk of the earth,
Reminders of laughter, and endless mirth.

Embracing Fleeting Petal Colors

I found some blooms in my old coat,
A bit of pink on my white boat.
They danced and swirled in the breeze,
Brought laughter mixed with pollen sneeze.

Crazy colors, a messy show,
Yellow here and a violet flow.
Fashion tips from flowers, no doubt,
Petal prints without a scout.

In pockets deep, a fragrant stash,
Who knew nature could bring such cash?
With every rustle and each hop,
I became a walking flower shop.

Forget my purse, it's just not fair,
When my pocket's a garden affair.
I strut in style, no worries on
With cheeky blooms till the break of dawn.

Gathered Remnants of the Day

After a stroll, what do I find?
Crumbs of nature left behind.
Yellow daffodils, pink blooms burst,
My secret garden, oh how I thirst!

I tuck them away like lost change,
Each one's story feels quite strange.
A mischievous flower bursts alive,
In my pocket, they jump and jive.

Crawling ants, they join the game,
A floral circus, who's to blame?
With petals sneaking under my sleeve,
They giggle as I try to weave.

Evening falls, my blooms take a seat,
In the pocket, quite the sweet treat.
I must confess, it gets quite wild,
When nature's mishaps leave me soiled.

Secrets in Floral Hues

Whispers of colors fill the air,
Hues so bright, I stop and stare.
A wink from red, a laugh from blue,
Secrets spoken in floral cues.

In my pocket, they sing and play,
A tiny party, come what may.
I shuffle along, join in the fun,
With jests and japes, we all run.

A lilac giggle, a daisy cheer,
Who knew flowers could be so dear?
They spill their tales of rain and sun,
In the pocket, life's just begun.

Now I'm known for my floral flair,
Like the secret keeper who doesn't care.
Each vibrant shade, a little jest,
Nature's laughter, simply the best.

Captured Essence of the Morning

Morning dawns, a fragrant start,
Sunshine and laughter, a blooming art.
My pockets hold every wild bloom,
An odd collection, a floral room.

With every bloom, a giggle, a wink,
They orchestrate chaos quicker than you think.
Bouncing about, they brighten my stride,
A pocket full of joy that I can't hide.

Morning glories tease with glee,
While daisies plot, just wait and see.
Together we giggle, frolic, and race,
A charming crew, keep up the pace!

As the sun climbs, blooms play their part,
Nature's jesters, a laugh at heart.
In my pocket, they spin and thrive,
A riot of joy, feeling alive!

The Space Between Petal and Heart

In a world where flowers hide,
I stow them all, a secret ride.
A daisy tickles, a rose slips in,
Giggles erupt from the chaos within.

Who knew that blooms could bring such cheer?
Inside my pockets, they whisper near.
A sneeze erupts, pollen on the loose,
A floral explosion, oh what a ruse!

Bouncing about, a sunflower grins,
While violets sing of whimsical sins.
Each little bud, a chuckle, a smile,
Nature's mischief, just my style!

Petals play tricks, like a cheeky elf,
Sometimes I wish they'd stay by themselves.
But in every fold, they find their way,
Turning my pockets into a flower buffet!

A Memory Book of Nature's Grace

Each crinkle and fold holds fragrant cheer,
A memory book, with petals here.
A pressed forget-me-not shows its face,
While I reminisce in this leafy space.

A daffodil tries to sneak a peek,
Sprouting laughter as I feel unique.
Sweet peas giggle, and roses tease,
Nature's scrapbook brings me to my knees!

Tulip tales and lily laughs,
Dance in pockets like quirky staffs.
Every leaf a story, every stem a song,
In this funny garden where I belong.

So if you find me with blooms galore,
Just remember, I'm always looking for more.
For the laughter of flowers fits time and pace,
In my secret diary of nature's grace!

Touched by Time's Soft Petals

Time plays tricks with petals so bright,
They flap and flutter, what a sight!
A butterfly winks, 'What's that you've got?'
I blush as I hold my secret plot.

Snippets of spring in my pocket maze,
Each one a memory, a funny phase.
Chasing a bee, I trip and roll,
Bells of laughter, my innocent goal.

With every petal, a giggle slips out,
Like confetti from my pocket, no doubt.
Time and petals, a comical dance,
Oh, how nature loves a good chance!

So next time you see an odd-looking chap,
With flowers in pockets and a silly clap,
Know I'm just touched by time's sweet jest,
Collecting laughter, and loving the fest!

Shards of Petal-Flecked Dreams

In a world of sunlit cheer,
I found a stash of blooms so dear.
A daisy danced with a bumblebee,
I laughed, 'What a sight for me!'

My pockets brimmed with colors bright,
A swirl of chaos, pure delight.
But when I sat to catch my breath,
Up popped a flower—insta-death!

I wore a cap, and let it fly,
The petals soared into the sky.
With every swish and every twirl,
I became the bloom-loving girl!

Now every step's a fragrant spree,
With loads of blooms following me.
My pockets, oh, they spill and spill,
A garden feast, against my will!

Bottled Sunshine of a Garden's Heart

Caught a gleam in a sunny jar,
Garden giggles weren't too far.
Tiny blooms in glass attire,
Swirl and sway like a merry choir.

Insects came for the sweet parade,
Each buzzing tune, a serenade.
I shook the bottle, what a mess,
Sunshine spilled—oh dear, I guess!

Butterflies joined in the fun,
"Let's dance away, we're never done!"
But then they got all mixed up too,
In shades of pink, and a dash of blue.

Now my garden's quite a sight,
A happening of pure delight.
Bottled sunshine, chaos galore,
Who needs calm? I'm wanting more!

A Pocket Full of Colorful Echoes

Deep in the seams of my old jeans,
Lurked whispers of what nature means.
A bluebell's voice, a rose's frown,
Echoes giggle, never drown.

Dandelions called, "Hey, come play!"
While I extracted them, in a fray.
Their wishes tickled my fancy feet,
Each step a dance, a flowery beat.

Onlookers chuckled, "What's that plight?"
A jester in a garden's light.
With every snag and little tear,
My colorful echoes filled the air.

Now my wardrobe's a leafy spree,
Fashion's best in petals free.
What used to be clothes now sounds a blast,
A pocket full of echoes, unsurpassed!

Worn Pages of a Flower's Journey

Once I penned a tale of blooms,
Bright adventures filled with fumes.
A sunflower smirked, "Let's play pretend!"
The stories laughed, my new best friends.

Worn pages told of zesty sights,
Petal play and joyful flights.
A clumsy bee with a crooked grin,
Buzzed right in, making quite a din!

Each chapter turned, the petals fluttered,
Through sunny fields, we joyfully uttered.
But my story ran out of space,
Paper flowers burst with grace!

Now scattered tales in every crease,
Worn pages bloom with zestful peace.
A flower's journey, oh what fun!
In each laugh, a bloom's just begun!

Tiny Treasures of Serenity

In my bag, I stow a wish,
Found a button, not a fish.
A soft rock, it feels so right,
For my dreams, it shines so bright.

A gum wrapper, oh so shiny,
A little squirrel called me whiny.
But with each trinket, I bring cheer,
Tiny joys are gathered near.

Leaves of Laughter

A crisp leaf danced upon my head,
'Twas a crown, as nature said.
With giggles soft, I wore it proud,
While the trees yelled, "Look, she's loud!"

A twig I found, a magic wand,
I cast a spell for fun, so grand.
And in the grass, I spotted ants,
The little ones in tiny pants.

Smiles of Bloom

A flower petal on my shoe,
It tickles me; I laugh anew.
The daisies giggle when I pass,
Suggesting I should join their class.

In this park, I'm quite the star,
Playing hopscotch with a jar.
Who knew blooms had such great wit?
In their world, I must admit.

The Unseen Garden Within

There's a garden in my head,
With rubber ducks and lots of bread.
Instead of flowers, there are dreams,
Silly thoughts flow like sunbeams.

A worm with shades and ice cream cone,
Wormy friends, we laugh and moan.
In this realm of fun and glee,
We plant a tree of creativity.

Whispers of Nature's Embrace

Trees whisper secrets in the breeze,
A butterfly laughs, 'Do as you please!'
I strolled along with silly flair,
Chasing clouds without a care.

A cheeky bird sang, 'Tap dance now!'
Before I knew it, I took a bow.
Nature's fun, within my reach,
With every step, joy's what I teach.

Blossoms Beneath the Surface

In my coat, a flower found,
A daisy, silly, round and sound.
I trip and laugh, it's quite absurd,
A rogue in pockets, who needs a bird?

They peek out when I sit to eat,
Cheering me up, they can't be beat.
A lily's leaf, a rose so bright,
My secret stash, a floral delight!

They dance around in laundry's spin,
Who knew my pockets held such whim?
A treasure trove of colors bold,
My fashion's tale in blooms retold.

So here I am with strange attire,
A petal cloak, my heart's desire.
Next time you laugh, just give a wink,
And check your pockets, don't you think?

The Archive of Floral Whispers

In an old jacket, secrets lay,
Whispers of blooms from yesterday.
A sunflower's giggle, a tulip's chat,
Every pocket holds a floral spat!

I pull one out, and it sneezes true,
Pollen mayhem, oh what a view!
My friends all snicker, they can't contain,
The daffodil's joke brings laughter and grain.

An archive filled with chuckles and cheer,
As blossoms gather, they draw near.
Telling stories of sunshine and rain,
A comedic twist on nature's gain.

So if you want a hearty laugh,
Just dip your hand in this fragrant half.
Among the petals, giggles rise,
A silly world in floral disguise.

A Tapestry of Nature's Keepsakes

Each flower tucked in pockets deep,
Promises of joy that make me leap.
A quirky quilt of colors bright,
Stitched with laughter, pure delight!

A marigold from a friend gone bold,
Whispers of mischief, tales untold.
A lilac whisper, soft and sweet,
My floral trove can't be beat!

Dandelions play hide and seek,
When I reach in, they burst with cheek.
Oh what fun a pocket can hold,
A garden of giggles, sunshine and gold.

So dance with me in a petal parade,
A tapestry woven, never to fade.
In pockets of laughter, we'll find our way,
Blooms that tickle and brighten the day.

Stains of Blossom on My Heart

A smudge of color, bright and bold,
A blossom's kiss, a tale retold.
On my shirt, the proof is clear,
A funny mishap, bring on the cheer!

With every spill, a giggle flies,
A floral blunder, a sweet surprise.
Carnations laugh with a mischievous poke,
As I stumble through life's fragrant joke.

In my head, the blooms are singing,
As petals dance, my heart's all swinging.
A floral spatter, a well-loved prank,
My wardrobe's charm, oh how it ranks!

So here I stand, with stains my pride,
A heart adorned in nature's guide.
Embrace the fun, let laughter sway,
In the gardens of joy, let's play away!

Stolen Fragrance

A scent escapes, I hold it close,
Like candy stolen, just not gross.
In grocery bags or pockets deep,
Each whiff a giggle, mine to keep.

A bloom I snatched from mom's bouquet,
She caught me laughing, forced to pay.
With every blossom, there's a tale,
Of fleshy pranks that never pale.

Hidden Hues

Bright colors packed, all snug and tight,
In pockets deep, they spark delight.
Surprise my friends with rainbow tricks,
A prank or two, just take your pick.

At school, I've hid them in my sock,
A secret stash, my own tick-tock.
They explode when laughter fills the air,
A palette dance, beyond compare.

Ephemeral Remnants of Spring

The blooms are gone, they made a dash,
Yet still I find a little stash.
A whimsy wafts from my inside,
Like jokes they play, I dare not hide.

As springtime flits like butterfly,
I chase the colors, oh me, oh my!
Each laugh a petal, soft and light,
Remembered moments shining bright.

The Weight of Delicate Gifts

Light as air, yet heavy too,
Hidden treasures, just for you.
I scoff at weight, my pockets bulge,
With laughter's weight, I feel them divulge.

Each bloom that's lost, a giggle's gain,
Wrapped in joy, they dance like rain.
With cheeks aglow, I share them wide,
These little laughs that swell with pride.

Hidden Bouquets of Memory

A bunch of giggles, tucked away,
In pockets deep, they long to play.
Unfolding laughter, softly bright,
    Reminiscing in the twilight.

When days grow dim, and smiles fade,
I pull them out, and they're remade.
Each silly thought, a flower's grace,
    A hidden bouquet in life's race.

Fleeting Whispers of Wildflowers

A daisy danced upon my shoe,
I laughed and said, "What's wrong with you?"
It twirled around like it was bold,
Saying, "I'm here! Let's break the mold!"

A sunflower winked with a grin,
It claimed it loved the chaos within.
I guess wildflowers have their way,
Of turning dull into a play!

Forget-me-nots giggled so light,
"We'll bloom and cause a little fright!"
In the pockets of giggles and cheer,
I found their whispers soft and clear.

So I embraced the earthy mess,
Nature's funny little dress.
With every bloom and silly joke,
I laughed until I nearly choked!

Treasure from the Lily's Heart

I met a lily with a secret stash,
Of shiny things and colorful flash.
"Tonight's the night for a treasure hunt,"
It winked at me, pulling a stunt!

With glimmers like stars in the sky,
I scoured the petals, oh my, oh my!
A shiny button, a lost earring too,
Nature's bounty is quite the view!

"In nature, there are gems galore!"
The lily cried, "Come explore some more!"
Wrapped in leaves and hidden in twirls,
Are forgotten things from distant worlds.

I gathered laughter and bits of fun,
With every trinket, I felt like a hun.
Oh, treasure is when laughter is sparked,
In the lily's heart, joy embarked!

Petal-Painted Journeys

I stuck some petals in my cap,
What a sight—a floral mishap!
As I strolled along the lane,
People pointed, tried not to feign.

"Is that a hat or a flowerbed?"
A toddler asked, tilting her head.
"A masterpiece of the wild," I grinned,
"Where laughter blooms and fun's unpinned!"

Bees buzzed loud, they thought I'm sweet,
Chasing me down the sunlit street.
With petals stuck, I danced and twirled,
Creating smiles in my little world.

At the park, they gathered 'round,
Compliments—like petals—dropped to the ground.
There's magic when you tease and play,
In a flower hat on a sunny day!

Collecting Nature's Confetti

In a garden, I spotted a spree,
Colors swirling, like a party!
With laughter loud and spirits bright,
The flowers danced with sheer delight.

I scooped up blooms in a little sack,
Each bright petal—I didn't hold back!
"It's nature's confetti, you see!"
I shouted like a happy bee!

A squirrel stared as I twirled,
"You're gathering fun? What a world!"
I handed him daisies with glee,
"Join the celebration, dance with me!"

Breezes blew, petals took flight,
We laughed and played into the night.
A garden party, oh, what a sight,
With nature's confetti, hearts feel light!

The Weight of Lush Reminders

I found some blooms, oh what a sight,
Stuffed in my jeans, they fit just right.
Every step I take, they spill and flop,
A floral parade, I just can't stop.

My friends all laugh, they point and tease,
"Why carry blooms? Just stick with cheese!"
But every flower has its own little tale,
Like being chased by a runaway snail.

I tried to stash them, hiding the stash,
But they escape and cause a splash.
In my socks, they do a jig,
This pocket garden, it's quite the gig!

Now I'm the king of floral flair,
With daisies hanging from my hair.
When it rains, oh what a mess,
A bloomin' fortune, I must confess!

Silhouettes of a Botanist's Heart

I'm no scientist, yet I still adore,
Collecting greens, but they start to soar.
One by one, they slip away,
"Hey, where'd you go?" I shout in dismay.

My shirt's a jungle, my socks a sea,
Floral accents, oh so free!
Each day a new fashion, I'm quite the sport,
Headed to work, and flowers report.

One time a rose took flight with grace,
Buzzing around, like it's in a race.
I tripped on a stem, fell flat on my face,
Now I'm a legend in this flower place!

With petals waving, they cheer and jeer,
My garden style, it brings great cheer.
"A botanist, you?" they all chime,
More like a florist caught in a mime!

A Hummingbird's Tender Touch

A swift little hum, oh what's that delight?
A hummingbird visit, it flits in sight.
But in my cap, it thinks there's a feast,
It zooms and swirls, like it's never ceased.

I swat at my head, what a strange thing,
A tiny green thief makes my heart sing.
"Hey buddy, or gal! Stick to the blooms,
Don't make my hat a nest of fumes!"

I duck and I dive, it darts with zeal,
As flowers bloom, it spins like a wheel.
A dance of the wings, so quick and spry,
I think it confused me with pie in the sky!

Now every time I hear that low hum,
I check my gloves, thinking, here it comes.
A buzz from the garden, it gives quite a show,
This feathered friend and I steal the flow!

Gentle Reminders Scattered About

The blooms don't care where they choose to land,
On coffee mugs or a slice of toast I planned.
In my cereal bowl, they swim with glee,
"Breakfast of flowers, come feast with me!"

Every drawer I open, there's more they find,
A secret stash, all intertwined.
"What's this?" says Mom, with a grin so sly,
"A floral confinement? Oh my, oh my!"

Tucked in my umbrella—oh, what a thrill!
They pop out, prancing, against my will.
I gather them quickly, with humor in mind,
A laugh for the day, joy of every kind.

So here's to the blooms, forever on spree,
Sprinkling mischief and giggles to me.
Like tiny confetti, they flitter about,
These gentle reminders, without a doubt!

The Color of Yearning Blooms

In my coat, a secret stash,
A burst of colors, oh so brash.
Daisies giggle, violets blush,
Each step I take, there's quite the rush.

Sunshine whispers, 'Do you care?'
While roses plot to take the air.
With each bloom, a quirky tale,
Of lost socks and a wobbly whale.

Laughter flutters in the breeze,
As dandelions dance with ease.
I trip and tumble, what a sight,
Wishing all my worries light.

So here's my garden, wild and bright,
A pocket full of sheer delight.
With every step, a chuckle grows,
In this wacky world where laughter flows.

Snippets of Wildflower Dreams

In the seams of my old jeans,
Blooming laughter, bursting seams.
Sunflowers wink with cheeky flair,
A bouquet's worth of playful air.

Petunias whisper, just for fun,
Tickling toes, a race to run.
Buttercups challenge my bright shoe,
'Catch me if you can!' they coo.

A stash of blooms, what luck I claim,
Pansies giggle at my name.
With every step, a silly twist,
A garden friend I can't resist.

So here I am, a walking spree,
Wildflower peace is chasing me.
With blossoms tumbling at my heels,
I welcome joy, with fancy reels.

Gathering Splendid Echoes

Echoes giggle 'neath my shirt,
Lavender sprinkles, how it flirts!
Each whiff a memory, sweet and bright,
Sending flowers into flight.

Daisies chant, 'We're quite the crew!'
While tulips plot to steal a shoe.
My pockets bulge, a blooming show,
With laughter hidden, just below.

As I stroll, they sing their tune,
A symphony beneath the moon.
With every step, a tickle toss,
Creating blooms from chaos, gloss.

So I gather, what a spree,
Echoes bursting wild and free.
With each petal, the stories grow,
A funny dance, this life's tableau.

Flutters of Scented Memories

In my purse, a secret stash,
Bottled giggles, quite the clash.
Whiffs of daisies, scent divine,
Turning moments into wine.

Sunshine chuckles through my hair,
As violets jump without a care.
Every swirl, a fragrant jest,
A floral joke, I must confess.

Twirling blooms with roots in dreams,
Dancing lightly, so it seems.
With every huff, a chuckle flows,
Creating laughter as it grows.

So here I stand, amidst the cheer,
Gathering scents that persevere.
In this garden, a funny muse,
Where every step ignites the blues.

Scented Memories in My Hands

Each flower's scent, a giggling tease,
Whispers of spring dance in the breeze.
With every whiff, a story spins,
Of bees that buzz and cheeky grins.

I cupped a daisy, a bit too tight,
It sneezed a pollen cloud, oh what a sight!
My sneeze echoed out with a loud "achoo!"
As petals flew, I laughed, did you?

A rose said, "Hey, don't crush my dreams!"
I apologized, but what about my schemes?
To hold the world in my warm palms,
And sprinkle joy like nature's balms!

So here I stand, a floral thief,
With floral laughter beyond belief.
Who knew that nature could be so sly?
With scented memories, I can surely fly!

Colors Caged in Silence

In a jar, they sit, the colors bright,
Each hue a secret, hidden from sight.
A mischievous bloom once tried to break free,
But it tangled with marigolds—oh, woe is me!

The violets giggle in their snug little space,
While dandelions roar, yearning for grace.
"Let us out for a dance!" they cry with glee,
But I chuckle, knowing they're too wild for me.

I opened the lid, and oh what a stir!
The colors erupted, a spontaneous blur.
Laughter erupted, and chaos ensued,
As daisies donned sunglasses, feeling quite shrewd!

So back in they went, all snug and cozy,
Funny how blooms can act so nosy.
Each color a character in a hilarious play,
A silent circus tucked away for the day!

A Scrapbook of Springtime

I gather the blooms like stories untold,
Creating a scrapbook, a treasure to hold.
Each page filled with laughs, I can't help but grin,
As nature's own laughter bursts from within.

A daffodil doodle, so bright and so bold,
It tickled my fingers, a sight to behold.
And tulips, they giggle in their rainbow hues,
Making up jokes that they happily choose.

I glue in a pansy that winked with delight,
Saying, "Life's too short, let's dance through the night!"
I chuckle and scribble the nuances sweet,
As blooms join the party with tiny, twinkling feet.

In my scrapbook, the laughter won't fade,
Each petal and leaf a delightful charade.
With memories fun, in pure joy I bask,
In the book of springtime, I'll never ask!

The Touch of Nature's Remnants

With bits of nature tucked in my coat,
I stride down the street, a giggling goat.
A leaf in my hair, a twig on my shoe,
Nature's fond tapping on a hilarious cue.

The squirrels they chuckle, judging my style,
As I prance about in my leafy file.
"Look at her go!" they say with a cheer,
A fashion statement—so wild and so dear!

A ladybug lands with a wink and a wave,
Trying to teach me to be quite brave.
"Dance like a flower, don't mind the crowd!"
And I twirl like the petals, feeling so proud.

In pockets of laughter, I carry the fun,
Nature's remnants, a wild-ridden run.
With giggles aplenty, I'll share through the day,
As the world around me dances in play!

Vignettes of Nature in Transit

A flower fished from the breeze,
Caught between my pocket's squeeze,
It giggles, flutters, starts to laugh,
At how it's now my silly scarf.

Dandelion seeds, a kid at play,
Blown kisses from the trees today,
They dance like they're in some grand ballet,
While I just watch and shout, 'Hooray!'

A leaf once bright, now dull and tired,
Sits in my wallet, once admired,
It whispers tales of summer's glow,
But now it's just a ticket, though!

In my shoe, a blossom shy,
It peeks out, oh so spry,
With roots entangled, oh what a mess,
Nature's way of saying, 'I confess!'

A Mosaic of Flora and Memories

Sunflowers wink as I walk by,
One belongs to my hair, oh my!
I strut with style, but they just grin,
Who knew that blooms could also spin?

A rogue daisy hides in my bag,
It dreams of sun while plotting a snag,
'Oh, I'll surprise your friend,' it brags,
And giggles while I fetch my rags.

Tiny violets in a game of seek,
They tickle my feet, making me squeak,
With laughter louder than any song,
This garden keeps our bond so strong.

My coat, it bears a leaf so bold,
It sways and dances, a sight to behold,
And as I stroll, it acts a fool,
Chasing butterflies, a jester at school.

Currents of Color Beneath My Skin

A giddy sprout beneath my sleeve,
Whispers secrets, won't believe!
It tickles my arm, oh what a thief,
This playtime from my floral belief.

An armful of petals starts to chatter,
'We're not just decor, we're here for laughter!'
They swing from my pockets, just like a clown,
Causing snickers all over town.

A mossy patch, feels like a hug,
Planting giggles in every rug,
As I tumble through this garden spree,
Nature's jesters, come laugh with me!

My shoes grow wild, a small bouquet,
With blooms that laugh at every sway,
Who knew that blossoms had such charm?
They smile at life, and sound the alarm.

Sketches of Softness and Light

In the fold of my shirt, a bloom does sprout,
It pokes and prods, 'Hey, let's go out!'
With laughter that's soft, it steals the show,
A dandelion's dream; where will we go?

A feathered petal floats by my ear,
With gossip of tulips, I draw it near,
It spins sweet stories of sunshine bright,
While I chuckle softly, feeling the light.

Buds in my hair create a fuss,
Whispering jokes, like 'Join the bus!'
They bounce with joy; oh what a ride,
Nature's bright jesters, I'm filled with pride.

With grass stains on my knees, oh dear!
A bouquet laughs, 'That's the best cheer!'
I stroll in softness, light as a kite,
With nature as my partner, oh what a sight!

Cradling the Fragrance of Youth

A whiff of spring, oh what a tease,
I dance with daisies, a laugh on the breeze.
With each bright bloom, I prance and play,
Who knew that youth could smell this way?

A lilac mishap, oh what a sight,
My hair is tangled in blue and white.
I'm a walking garden, a funny affair,
With bees and butterflies caught in my hair!

Nature's Remnants on My Sleeve

A leaf that clings to my favorite shirt,
Tells tales of adventures, mud, and dirt.
I'm sporting twigs like a casual trend,
Fashion advice from a squirrel, my friend!

A tiny snail left a trail, oh so slick,
I'll claim it's a style, my trendy trick.
With petals caught in my elbow's fold,
My fashion sense? Well, it's bold!

Bottling the Breath of Gardens

Caught a whiff of a rose so divine,
Decided to bottle it, feeling just fine.
But the top slipped off, oh look at me now,
A fragrant disaster, I'll take a bow!

Jars of delights all lined on my shelf,
With scents of my mischief, just being myself.
Caught in a giggle, I trip and I spill,
This garden of smells is giving me thrills!

Seasons Worn on Gentle Hands

My fingers are stained with autumn's embrace,
Clumsily wearing leaves, what a silly grace.
Dropping acorns like they're confetti galore,
In my festival of fall, who could want more?

A winter's touch with snowflakes aglow,
I catch them all, in a playful throw.
But as they melt, they start to drip down,
I've turned into a soggy, giggling clown!

Fragmented Moments of Floral Delight

A daisy danced upon my shoe,
Its petals giggling, yes, it's true.
I waved hello, it waved back fast,
In that moment, my worries passed.

A buttercup hid in my hair,
It tickled me with floral flair.
I laughed so loud it caught a bee,
What a wild, sweet melody!

In a jar the lilacs sway,
Catching sunlight, come what may.
They whispered jokes from long ago,
And left me chuckling, don't you know?

So here I roam with blooms around,
My pockets full of joy profound.
Each flower's whim brings giggles bright,
Fragmented moments of sheer delight.

Soft Prints of Blossoms Past

A rose once told me, "Ain't it grand?"
"I'm not just pretty, I'm in demand!"
I rolled my eyes and took a seat,
As petals fell, they looked so sweet.

The tulips chimed in, laughed in glee,
They made a ruckus, oh so free.
"I once wore shoes of butter and cream,"
They teased each other, like in a dream.

Daffodils burst with sunny jokes,
Said, "We're the best of leafy folks!"
I clutched my sides, for they were sly,
Soft prints of laughter echoing by.

With every petal that I find,
I sense their joy, a funny kind.
Blossoms past, a giggling spree,
In my pocket, wild jubilee!

The Keepsake of Spring's Caress

Spring bestowed with light-hearted cheer,
A bouquet whispered, "I'm a souvenir!"
I tucked it close, oh what a thrill,
A little laughter, a burst of will.

My friend the fern, with fronds so spry,
Told jokes of leaves that dared to fly.
"Watch me twirl in the breeze so free!"
I joined the dance, just wait and see.

With blooms that told tales, colorful lore,
Each petal chuckled, never a bore.
The keepsake cherished, with silly glee,
Spring's caress wrapped in jubilee.

So I prance with flowers, oh what a sight,
In laughter's embrace, everything feels right.
A bouquet of giggles, forever to bask,
In moments cherished, oh what a task!

Tales of Wilting Whispers

In the corner sat a dandy bloom,
Telling tales that filled the room.
"Why are we wilting? What's the fuss?"
The others giggled, "Join the bus!"

With stories of puffs and sunny beams,
They spun wild yarns of dandelion dreams.
"Caught in the wind, we had a spree,
An adventure bold, just wait and see!"

The petunias chipped in, soft yet sly,
"Remember the day we tried to fly?"
Laughter erupted, petals all around,
A blooming chorus, a vibrant sound.

For wilting whispers aren't all doom,
They tell of life, of joy in bloom.
In pockets they linger, memories bright,
Tales of laughter, soft, and light.

Keepsakes of the Wandering Breeze

A gust snatched my sandwich, oh dear,
Flying away like a trickster, I fear.
It twirled past the trees with a mischievous glee,
Leaving me hungry, with crumbs on my knee.

A swirl of loose change danced in the air,
Like pennies from heaven, beyond my despair.
I laughed at the chaos, a money parade,
Oh, how the wind loves its wild charade.

My hat took a trip, flew high like a kite,
I chased it with laughter, what a silly sight.
In the chase, I found a leaf, green and spry,
With stories unspoken, like birds in the sky.

Yet memories linger, each gust brings a smile,
For laughter and breezes go hand in hand, style.
In pockets of joy, I gather the breeze,
Each whimsy encounter, my heart's sweet tease.

Touching the Essence of Daisies

I picked a bouquet of daisies so bright,
But they played hide and seek, what a delight!
They danced in the garden, all close in a throng,
I thought I was right, but I guess I was wrong.

With each tiny stem, a giggle emerged,
As bees buzzed around, my confusion surged.
I thought I was crafty, a flower thief bold,
But the blooms whispered secrets, stories untold.

They told me of sunshine, of raindrops and dew,
Of squirrels in tuxedos, all dressed up for a brew.
I shared a few laughs with my new flowery friends,
Though many, like me, thought this fun would not end.

So accompanied by daisies, I pranced through the day,
With nature's pure mischief, tossing worries away.
I tucked them in pockets, they chuckled with glee,
For life's little follies are best shared in spree.

The Weight of Graceful Moments

I tripped on a daffodil, oh what a blunder,
Landed in a patch, now that's true wonder!
With petals like blankets, so soft and so warm,
I rolled like a tumbleweed, oh what a charm!

Butterflies laughed at the sight of my flail,
As they danced around me, with grace they set sail.
I swore I could hear them, gossiping fair,
About me, the klutz, with flowers in my hair.

Each step I took echoed a crinkle, a crunch,
Like a hidden bag of chips at lunchtime's brunch.
The blooms kept their secrets as I stumbled about,
In nature's embrace, I let laughter shout.

So here's to the moments, unplanned and absurd,
Where grace meets the silly, in laughter unheard.
With blossoms as witnesses, we cheerfully roam,
For life's little quirks make the best kind of home.

Traces of Nature's Tender Heart

A raindrop waltzed down my nose, what a tease,
It tickled my laughter and danced with the breeze.
Each droplet was playful, a jester of sorts,
Leaving trails of sunshine, in quaint water ports.

A squirrel stole my snack, with a cheeky grin,
As I watched in disbelief, my laughter did spin.
He then offered a acorn, a trade for some crumbs,
I accepted, delighted, as humorance hums.

The flowers were gossiping, they had tales to share,
Of bumbles and fumbles, with petals to spare.
Each whisper cascaded like giggles from vine,
In nature's grand jest, life lovingly twines.

So here I will sit, with friends blooming bright,
Together in whimsy, we banish the blight.
For traces of laughter make memories bloom,
In pockets of joy, they burst forth like perfume.

Whispers of Blooming Secrets

In a jacket, blooms I hide,
A secret stash, they can't abide.
Petunias prance, daffodils tease,
My pocket garden, the ultimate breeze.

With each step, they rattle and jive,
Floral dancers, so alive.
Neighbors peek, then turn away,
What do they think? Do they want to play?

Fragments of Floral Dreams

A daisy here, a rose is there,
Laughter lingers in the air.
I trip on stems while skipping bliss,
Who knew flowers could cause such a mess?

A snapdragon pokes my side so sly,
'It's just us two!' it seems to cry.
We strut and sway, become a scene,
In this floral frolic, we're all so keen.

A Tapestry of Fragile Moments

Floral notes in my pants, oh dear,
When I bend down, things disappear!
Sunflowers giggle, their heads so high,
As I become a walking bouquet, oh my!

Every flower, a whisper, a tale,
Short of a garden but never stale.
I play the fool, they play along,
Together, we craft a jolly song.

Secrets Scattered in Bloom

Behind my back, they're plotting a spree,
An action-packed, floral jubilee!
Hyacinths chuckle, tulips roll in glee,
Turning my pockets into a flower spree.

Oh what a ruckus, oh what a sight,
Blossoms exploding in pure delight.
With petals flying in every direction,
Who knew pockets could hold such perfection?

A Dance with Withering Leaves

Leaves twirl and twist in the air,
Dancing like they just don't care.
One lands on my head with a flip,
I laugh as it takes a quick trip.

Squirrels are plotting their autumn heist,
Stealing acorns, oh how they feast!
A leaf scolds me for being too slow,
But who knew grass could steal the show?

Wind whispers jokes in the trees,
As I giggle and stumble with ease.
Nature's humor, a sly little tease,
Tickles my funny bone, I can't help but sneeze.

The sun winks at me from the skies,
While daisies chuckle in rainbow ties.
With every step, I'm losing my grace,
Who knew autumn could be such a race?

Fleeting Tales of the Meadow's Kiss

In the meadow where the daisies play,
Butterflies barter for a sunny stay.
The grass tickles my toes as they flee,
And bumbles buzz louder, oh how carefree!

A ladybug leads a parade with flair,
While ants are juggling with great care.
"Watch your step!" they call with glee,
But who could tread lightly near such jubilee?

Clouds race above like they're late for lunch,
While crickets chirp a rhythmic munch.
The bluebells giggle, their voices a tease,
Inviting me to join their playful breeze.

I chase a dream, a whimsical flight,
But trips on petals bring laughter to light.
In nature's embrace, I lose all fear,
As memories bloom like flowers, oh dear!

Whispered Stories of Nature's Palette

The trees gossip with a flickering sound,
As flowers gossip 'round and around.
A dandelion makes a wish on the breeze,
While bees share secrets with such great ease.

Silly shadows dance in the glow,
A rabbit stumbles, oh what a show!
With grass stains on fur, it gives a grin,
Who knew nature could be such a win?

Petunias play peek-a-boo 'neath the sun,
"Lettuce take a break, we've had our fun!"
A sunflower mocks in a towering way,
Mimicking the clouds in a playful sway.

Even the rocks tell tales of their plight,
Mocking the squirrels, oh what a sight!
Laughter erupts from the roots of a tree,
As honeybees buzz, "Come dance with me!"

A Soft Reverie Stitched in Time

In the quiet moments where dreamers play,
A patchwork of memories sewn every day.
Buttons of laughter, stitches of cheer,
Pinning the giggles that hover near.

Sunlight weaves through the branches so sly,
While shadows whisper and giggle, oh my!
The breeze brushes softly, a tickling sigh,
As daisies wear hats, just to comply.

Time hops along on bunnies' soft feet,
While dandelions burst into the heat.
"What's the hurry?" the daisies cry,
As they twirl in the wind, just passing by.

Every flower's laughter, a soft serenade,
Leaves me wondering how time has played.
With petals unfolding, stories take flight,
In a colorful reverie, all feels just right.

Chronicles of a Season's End

As autumn leaves begin to fall,
I find my socks are filled with them all.
They're playful jesters in hues so bright,
My laundry's an art show, what a sight!

I dance through piles, a leafy spree,
A crunching symphony just for me.
With every step, a rustling cheer,
Nature's confetti, oh so dear!

I marvel at my colorful fate,
Turn fashion blunders into great art,
Gold and brown, a strange costume,
It's a fashion choice none could presume!

So here's to endings, bold and loud,
A closet of laughter, I'm quite proud.
In pockets, surprises tucked away,
Who knew nature could add such play?

Fragrance in the Quiet Hour

In moments hush, when all seems still,
I smell a whiff of an odd thrill.
Did I just catch a whiff of cheese?
Or is that lavender in the breeze?

A bouquet stashed in my old coat,
With tiny things that make me gloat.
That time I thought I'd bake a pie,
Lost in my sleeves, a wild surprise!

Each scent tells tales of clumsy days,
Of snacks I hoarded in funny ways.
A cinnamon stick, a sprig of thyme,
These pockets hold smells that are sublime!

So if you sniff and find a snack,
Justremember it's part of the pack.
Laughter waits in every corner,
In the quiet hour, let joy reign warmer!

Of Dried Blooms and Memories

In my pockets, a dusty bouquet,
Forgotten flowers still want to play.
A rose of July, now crispy and dry,
It's crumbled charm makes me laugh and sigh.

Once a lover's gift, now a joke,
A fragrant memoir that just won't poke.
Petals that whispered sweet nothings now,
Put a smile on my face, take a bow!

With each motley piece, it's quite clear,
Memories linger, refuse to disappear.
Old love letters, and odd charms too,
They colored my life in vibrant hues.

So here's to the blooms that time forgot,
With humor they've brought, it's quite a lot.
Dried and crumpled, yet still full of cheer,
They make me chuckle when I draw near!

The Hidden Palette of My Skirt

My skirt a canvas, colors not planned,
A rainbow mishap from a messy hand.
With candy wrappers and crumbs galore,
Each tiny piece tells tales of yore.

The blues from berries, green from grass,
This patchwork art, I'm proud to amass.
A dollop of mustard, a stitch of thread,
The life I lead in colors spread.

I twirl and giggle, a spin-n-splash,
Every flutter catches light with a dash.
A colorful jingle, a whimsical breeze,
Who knew my wardrobe would aim to please?

So friends, don't judge my dress of fate,
It's a wearable laugh, don't hesitate.
In every fold, a secret tucked tight,
A vibrant story in the sunlight!

Sprigs of Nostalgia in Silken Air

In a garden, I once roamed,
Where daisies danced, and bees once combed.
A butterfly stole my lunch one day,
And flew off laughing, hip-hip-hooray!

With tulips tall, I tried to climb,
But tripped on roots, oh what a crime!
Laughter echoed through the green,
As I discovered how grass can lean.

A ladybug became my friend,
On my shoulder, she'd daily pretend.
We shared secrets, just her and me,
Until she flew off, so wild and free!

Memories swirl, like petals in air,
Tickling my thoughts, with light-hearted flair.
Each moment a giggle, each scent a grin,
In my heart's pocket, nostalgia begins!

A Symphony of Color Beneath My Skin.

Colors in my closet collide,
A rainbow fight, nowhere to hide.
Wearing orange with purple socks,
I wonder if I've lost my rocks!

The blue shirt shrieks, 'Dress to impress!'
While the green pants fearfully confess,
That their last dance was quite absurd,
With polka dots making quite a blur!

A melody of mismatched flair,
Exclaims a sweet, floral affair.
Each outfit's a joke, a laugh, a spin,
Beneath my skin, let the fun begin!

In closets wild, where hues collide,
Life's symphony plays, none can deride.
With each step, I prance and sway,
Who knew fashion could be such a play?

Whispers of Abandoned Blooms

In the field, where daisies faded,
I stumbled upon flowers jaded.
"Why so sad?" I gently inquired,
"We were once vibrant, now we're retired!"

The roses sighed, "We've had our day,
But the sun forgot to shine our way.
We used to blush in the breezy light,
Now we're just gossiping all night!"

With petals down, they wear their loss,
The bees ignore them, what a toss!
"Make a wish," said a dandelion,
And I hoped for blooms to join the lion!

So I gathered them, with twinkling eyes,
Whispered, "Time to re-write your skies!"
In a vase, they laughed, oh what a croon,
Abandoned blooms found their fortune soon!

Secrets of the Fragile Fragrance

There's a bottle with scent from way back when,
A mix of giggles and moments in pen.
But each spritz smells like my grandma's stew,
I wonder if she added a secret or two!

Lilacs whisper in dreams of June,
While my perfume hums a silly tune.
With hints of laughter and mischief in play,
It smells like joy on a bright sunny day!

A whiff of roses gets me to grin,
While minty freshness invites me to spin.
"Why not combine us?" the flowers declare,
"Let's create chaos with scents in the air!"

So I douse myself, a fragrant delight,
Transforming each moment, igniting the night.
In a world full of scents, I'll dance and prance,
With secrets of fragrance, I take my chance!

The Symphony of Silky Skirts

A twirl and a whirl, oh what fun,
The skirts dance around like they're on the run.
They rustle and giggle, a playful delight,
Chasing the breeze, both day and night.

In my wardrobe they jive, all colors and hues,
A party of fabrics, oh what a ruse!
One slip on the floor, I now start to slide,
A carnival of laughter, I can't seem to hide.

Skirts whisper secrets, they shush and they sigh,
As I try to keep calm, but oh, my oh my!
They tangle my legs, it's a comedy show,
With each frolicsome flap, I trip like a pro.

So let's raise a ruckus, a skirted parade,
With every twirl, let mischief invade.
In this whimsical world of whimsical twirls,
I'm the queen of the chaos, all giggles and swirls.

Tethered to the Earth's Craft

Tangled in twine, a crafter's delight,
My fingers are dancing, from morning to night.
With glue on my nose and paint on my chin,
Every small project's a journey to win!

The yarn has a mind, it knots up my fate,
A bird's nest of colors, oh, just look at that state!
In my box of mishaps, creativity thrives,
Each stitch tells a story, that foolishness jives.

Scissors might giggle, as they dart out to play,
I snip and I snatch, in a crafty ballet.
My glue stick's a hero, but sometimes a foe,
And glitter's the villain that steals every show.

So here's to the art, and all of its quirks,
To messes and marvels, to all of its perks.
With laughter we build, with joy we collapse,
In this wild dance of crafting mishaps.

Shadows of Marigold Memories

In the garden they giggle, those blossoms so bright,
Whispering tales of a joyous delight.
With petals like ribbons, fluttering free,
A parade in the sun, oh look at them flee!

I chase them to dusk, through twirls and through shouts,
And trip on the roots of the fun little sprouts.
Each shadow that hops, hides laughter from view,
As I tumble and tumble, in colors so true.

These flowers speak stories, of time gone awry,
Of bees with their banter, and butterflies sly.
They beckon me closer, with scents oh so sweet,
In this marigold dance, I'm light on my feet!

So let's paint the skies with the sun's glowing rays,
And cherish the moments, these whimsical days.
For shadows that linger, a chuckle they bring,
In the garden of laughter, we plant dreams that sing.

The Quiet of a withered Rose

A wilted old dame, with petals so crinkled,
In a vase on the shelf, her glory's now sprinkled.
Yet with every crunch, there's a secret she shares,
Of romance and roses, of love's playful snares.

She sighs of the past, with a wise little grin,
As I ponder her tales of where she has been.
"Oh sweet child," she mutters, "don't you wish you could see,
The mischief of blooms, in their heyday carefree?"

The dust gathers softly, like memories sweet,
While I laugh at her stories, each one a heartbeat.
Though faded she seems, with elegance bold,
Her laughter still dances, a beauty untold.

So here's to the withered, the frayed and the grey,
For wisdom in silence, shines brighter than play.
In a world full of blooms, it's the quiet that grows,
The laughter of life, in a withered rose.

Echoes of Blossom's Lament

A flower sneezed, oh what a sight,
Flew through the air, landing just right.
Daisies danced in a silly parade,
With hijinks galore, their antics displayed.

A bee got dizzy, buzzing around,
Crashing into petals that fluttered down.
In a whirlwind of color, they twirled and spun,
Who knew nature could be such fun?

But then I tripped on a rogue daffodil,
And fell face-first, through sheer will.
Yet laughter erupted, pure as can be,
From the flowers mocking, just wait and see!

So if you find blooms in your hair,
Know they threw a party without a care.
With every sneeze and silly prank,
These flowers of mischief deserve their rank.

Stolen Moments of Blooming Beauty

Sneaking blooms from the neighbor's bush,
Like a rogue thief in a floral rush.
I slipped and tumbled, landed with grace,
Covered in petals, my bright red face.

A rose whispered secrets, soft as a sigh,
'That's how you ruin a garden, oh my!'
I waved goodbye, gave a sheepish grin,
Who knew such joy could come from a sin?

The tulips giggled, heads held high,
As I clutched handfuls, running nearby.
In every stash of stolen bloom,
Lives a moment that brightens the gloom.

With flower crowns crafted by sheer delight,
I wore my treasures as day turned to night.
Every stolen glance became a cheer,
For beauty that bloomed when laughter was near.

A Pocketful of Forgotten Gardens

In my pocket, a garden exists,
With daisies and wishes and silly twists.
A lilac's whisper, a peony sigh,
They giggle and wiggle when I pass by.

Yet the dandelions plot with wild schemes,
To burst from my pocket, living their dreams.
'A wildflower riot,' they plan on a spree,
To take over my socks and share tea with me.

I reached for a snack, found a rose instead,
With petals like laughter, I thought, 'What a spread!'
But bread and butter aren't flowers, agree?
Hence lunch became nature's glorious spree.

So here I sit with a pocketful of glee,
While my "flower garden" rebels against me.
Every bloom a partner in playful theft,
In the pockets of joy, it's flowers we've left.

The Beauty I Carry

In a bag of wonders, flowers take flight,
With quirks and oddities, bloom day and night.
Sunflowers giggle at cloudy tales,
While violets whisper in shimmery veils.

Each bloom a treasure, a story to tell,
Of garden adventures and mischief as well.
Roses pretending to blush with grace,
While daisies argue who takes up space.

Yet all these blooms keep me feeling bright,
With laughter and color that feels just right.
So here's to the beauty that flowers bestow,
In pockets or bags, wherever we go.

So if you see a flower spill and smile,
Know it's just friends being silly awhile.
Laughing and singing with all of their might,
Creating a joy that's pure and polite.

A Handful of Colorful Reminiscence

In my little pouch, blooms do collide,
An army of colors, a whimsical ride.
I pull out a daisy, it giggles and spins,
And off we go dancing, as laughter begins.

A rose tucked away, oh the prickle it lends,
It tickles my fingers as it pretends.
A tulip joins in, wearing shades of delight,
Together we chuckle, oh what a sight!

A daffodil joins, in a snappy parade,
It quips about sunshine, not wanting to fade.
In my vibrant stash, a party in store,
With each little bloom, I can't help but roar!

So here in my pocket, let whimsy delight,
Where flowers are friends, and humor takes flight.
In this garden of giggles, all troubles can cease,
A handful of memories, a pocket of peace.

Harvesting Hope from the Ground

I dug in the dirt with a shovel so bright,
Hoping for treasures, or maybe a bite.
What sprouted was laughter, oh what a surprise,
A carrot with glasses, that squinted its eyes.

An onion start crying, I offered a joke,
It giggled and snorted, then added some smoke.
A tomato in blush, said, 'Don't catch a chill!'
We're growing together, let's plant our goodwill!

A beet with a grin, declared it a feast,\nWhile zucchinis waved, like a friendly beast.
Each harvest a chuckle, we celebrate cheer,
With veggies and humor, let's spread it right here.

So in this rich soil, what love we have found,
With laughter as fertilizer, joy's all around.
Let's nurture the funny, with sunshine and care,
Harvesting hope in the garden we share.

Fragrant Echoes of Enchantment

In my jacket, surprises, sweet scents like a dream,
A whiff of fresh laughter, where fairies all scheme.
An orange with giggles, a lemon with cheer,
Each fruity encounter brings smiles oh so near.

A sprig from the mint, it tickles my nose,
Inviting a dance under skies like a rose.
A whiff of mischief, a tease in the air,
As flowers eavesdrop, with giggles to spare.

A cinnamon twist, it winks with delight,
Stirring up memories, everything's right.
With echoes of laughter, I skip through the day,
In the world of sweet aromas, fun leads the way.

So here's to the magic that scents can evoke,
The laughter, the joy, the warmth of each joke.
In fragrant enchantment, together we soar,
With each chuckle blooming, forever, we roar!

Delicate Dreams Under Canvas Sky

Beneath a wide canvas, painted in hues,
I toss out my dreams like confetti, amuse.
A cloud made of cotton candy floats by,
It laughs as it drifts, saying, 'Oh, do try!'

A shooting star giggles, slides down for a chat,
Says, 'Wishes are funny, just look where they're at!'
A sprinkle of stardust tickles my toes,
While moonbeams engage in a dance that just grows.

Balloons filled with chuckles are drifting away,
As fireflies flicker, they join in to play.
Each dream whispers softly, wrapped up in delight,
Under this canvas, the world feels so light.

So here in the night, let's giggle and scheme,
With delicate wishes, we'll follow each dream.
Under a cosmic canvas, we frolic and fly,
In twilight's embrace, our laughter won't die.

www.ingramcontent.com/pod-product-compliance
Lightning Source LLC
Chambersburg PA
CBHW070309120526
44590CB00017B/2604